DEMCO

MAGNIFICENT HORSES OF THE WORLD

ARABIAN HORSES

For a free color catalog describing Gareth Stevens' list of high-quality books, call 1-800-542-2595 (USA) or 1-800-461-9120 (Canada). Gareth Stevens' Fax: (414) 225-0377.

Library of Congress Cataloging-in-Publication Data available upon request from publisher.
Fax: (414) 225-0377 for the attention of the Publishing Records Department.

ISBN 0-8368-1367-7

This edition first published in North America in 1995 by
Gareth Stevens Publishing
1555 North RiverCenter Drive, Suite 201
Milwaukee, Wisconsin 53212, USA

First published in Great Britain in 1994 by Sunburst Books, Deacon House, 65 Old Church Street, London, SW3 5BS.
Photographs © 1989 Franckh'sche Verlagshandlung, W. Keller & Co., Stuttgart, Germany. Text © 1994 Sunburst Books.
Additional end matter © 1995 by Gareth Stevens, Inc.

U.S. Series Editor: Patricia Lantier-Sampon
U.S. Editor: Barbara J. Behm

Printed in China

1 2 3 4 5 6 7 8 9 99 98 97 96 95

MAGNIFICENT HORSES OF THE WORLD

ARABIAN HORSES

Photography by
Tomáš Míček

Text by
Dr. Hans-Jörg Schrenk

Gareth Stevens Publishing
MILWAUKEE

Arabians are small horses with broad heads, wide nostrils, and large eyes set far apart.

Arabian mares with their foals. It is only when Arabian horses are in full motion that the true beauty of these thoroughbreds can be seen.

An elegant Arabian mare. Arabian thoroughbreds are regarded as the purest breed of horse in the world.

Arabian horses are known for their beauty, stamina, and strength. These features have earned them the admiration and adoration of horse lovers everywhere.

Arabians are the oldest purebred horses in the world, and no other horse has had such a great influence on so many other breeds. Over the course of centuries, the Arabian has been used to develop Andalusians, Lipizzaners, English thoroughbreds, and Trakehners, and has been used to improve the blood of almost every breed. The offspring produced from such crossbreeding are usually larger than the Arabian horse itself.

A graceful Arabian thoroughbred enjoys springtime in a poppy field. Arabians have concave, or "dished," faces. Their manes and tails are fine-haired and silky.

The Arabian horse is an ancient breed that originated in the Middle East. The ancestors of today's Arabians were the wild horses of the highlands in central Asia. As long ago as 2000 B.C., horses from this region lived on the fertile plain between the Nile and Euphrates rivers. But some historians believe this breed has inhabited the Arabian peninsula since 5000 B.C. One prehistoric rock drawing dating back more than 8,000 years shows a horse with Arabian features.

The ruler of Israel from 972-922 B.C., King Solomon, captured Arabian horses from Egypt and the Arabian deserts. His stables housed more than forty thousand Arabians.

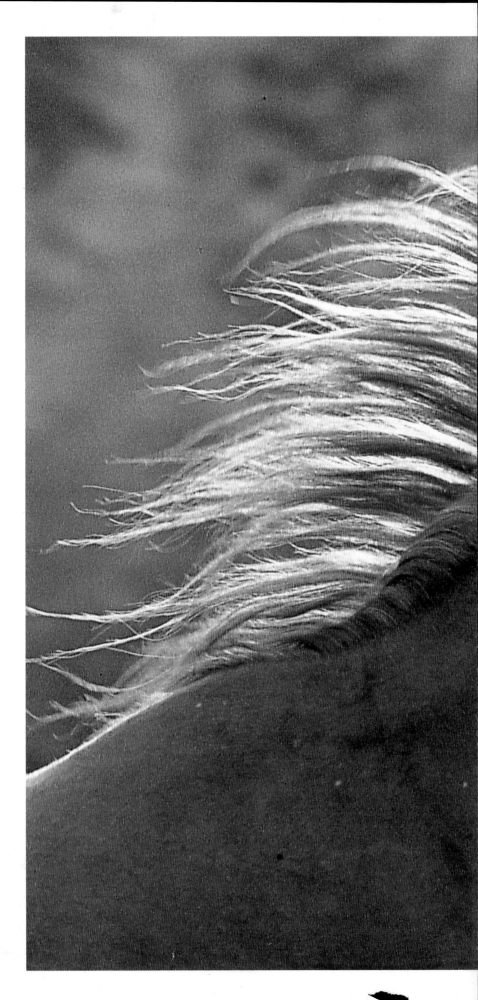

A chestnut mare. Arabian horses commonly have chestnut, bay, gray, white, or black coats.

A herd of mares. Arabians are known as the "daughters of the wind."
They have short backs; prominent chests and hindquarters;
and thin, small-boned legs.

In the second century A.D., the nomadic Bedouin tribes of the Arabian desert began breeding these horses. The Bedouins desired a horse that was beautiful, yet tough enough to survive the desert. They carefully bred the Arabian horse for centuries, making sure the line was kept pure.

Although the horse breeding practices of the Bedouins played an important role in the development of the breed, today's Arabians are quite different from the ancient Arabian horse. The Arabian of today developed throughout later centuries. The features of the modern Arabian horse were shaped by harsh desert conditions, including a sparse food supply, extreme temperatures, and terrible sand storms. Only the strongest horses could survive the hostile conditions. The weak and vulnerable horses died out. The desert toughened the Arabian survivors, giving them even greater strength and stamina than the ancient horses.

A young chestnut stallion enjoys a fragrance that has filled the air.

Arabian horses are one of the finest racehorse breeds in the world. They are graceful, trim, and hardy. They move quickly and lightly on their feet, and they can run for long distances with great endurance.

A gray mare spends some quality time with her foal in a spring pasture.

Fiery and athletic Arabians release pent-up energy in a series of leaps and bounds.

Two beautiful brood
mares enjoy a field
of flowers.

Arabians are the most widespread breed of horse in the world.

This stallion descended from a strong line of Spanish Arabian horses.

Arabian horses are famous for their elegance and speed. Their chests are broad and muscular, and their tails are set high.

27

An Arabian mare and her foal. Arabians are often considered the most beautiful of all the horses. They are also known for their longevity.

The founder of the religion called Islam, the prophet Muhammed, contributed to the breeding of Arabian horses starting in the early A.D. 600s. Muhammed wanted to spread the word of Islam throughout the world. He also wanted to establish a worldwide Arabian empire. He knew this could only be achieved with a powerful army mounted on purebred horses. Muhammed, therefore, ordered the breeding of noble and pure horses. He promised the reward of life in paradise after death to every person who raised and donated such a horse for the cause. He said, "However many grains of barley you give to your horse, this is the number of sins which you will be forgiven all at once."

The Muslim army made its way through Egypt, North Africa, across the Mediterranean, and into Spain and France, conquering all in its path. But the Muslims eventually were defeated. They returned to their homelands, leaving many of their magnificent horses behind. This stock was the beginning of the Arabian influence on the native horses of Europe.

In Spain, Arabian stallions were crossed with the native mares. The result of this crossbreeding was the Andalusian horse. The Andalusian was introduced into many European countries for breeding to refine the existing stock of heavy, bulky horses.

In the many wars that took place in Europe during the sixteenth, seventeenth, and eighteenth centuries, Arabian horses proved to be superior over native breeds. Two great promoters of the Arabian were Louis XV and Napoleon. Following his Russian defeat, Napoleon and his officers were only able to flee back to France thanks to the stamina of their Arabian horses. All the other types of horses fell victim to the cold and the stresses of war. European rulers realized that the way to improve the native breeds was to crossbreed with the Arabian.

They acquired Arabian stallions to crossbreed with the native mares. At that time, little thought was given to the idea of pure Arabian breeding. Only a few wealthy buyers, such as King Wilhelm I, took part in the breeding of pure Arabian stock.

Arabian horses from the region of Egypt date back to 2000 B.C. This line was protected and promoted by Abbas Pasha, the Viceroy of Egypt from 1848-1850. The offspring of his horses are some of the best of the Arabian breed in existence today.

Arabians have prominent foreheads. Their small ears are alert and curved.

*Two Arabian colts have a first meeting in a meadow. Even the colts
have the finely chiseled facial features for which
Arabians are famous.*

If foals do not have playmates their own age, they try to persuade their mothers into having some fun with them.

Arabians are no longer bred as the hardy, high-performance horses once needed by the military. But Arabians used in today's sporting activities do require special breeding to prevent them from becoming too heavy and cumbersome. This allows the horses to move with fast, seemingly effortless strides. The gallop is their natural pace. The Arabians also have the strength and endurance to keep a fast pace for long periods of time.

Arabians are bred throughout the world, and almost every modern breed has Arabian ancestors. The international breeding of Arabian thoroughbreds is an attempt to preserve a tradition that is in danger of dying out in its very own homeland. After all, in the deserts of central Arabia, there are no longer roving Bedouin tribes mounted on pure, swift horses. Many of today's Bedouins drive cars and make a living selling oil.

Arabians have noble heads and long, arched necks. They are affectionate, intelligent, and graceful.

A Spanish Arabian and her young foal.
Arabians are elegantly proportioned.

Arabians are no longer used in war and conquest. People now enjoy them for leisure and relaxation, taking part in activities such as showing, racing, and riding. In addition, horses that are crossbred with Arabians improve in these areas. They, too, become faster, more agile and spirited, and have more stamina.

The original Arabians were chestnut and bay. Now they can be found in many colors, especially gray.

A gray Spanish stallion. This photograph provides a clear view of the large, dark eyes of the Arabians, known as the "Spanish eye."

Arabians are proud and courageous. They move with the head and tail held high and ears alert. The gallop is the natural pace of these horses.

Arabians are spirited horses, but they also are peaceful and gentle.

GLOSSARY

bay — reddish brown in color.

breed — animals having specific traits; to produce offspring.

chestnut — reddish brown in color.

colts — male horses under the age of four years.

crossbreeding — the mating of a male of one breed with a female of another.

foals — newborn male or female horses.

gallop — a fast way of running by an animal, such as a horse.

herd — a number of animals of one kind that stay together and travel as a group.

longevity — having a long life.

manes — the long hair around the necks of horses.

mares — female horses.

nomadic — continually traveling from one place to another.

offspring — the young produced by a pair of animals.

stallions — mature male horses used for breeding.

stamina — endurance or staying power.

thoroughbred — a horse or another animal that is bred from the best blood through a long line.

MORE BOOKS ABOUT HORSES

Album of Horses. Marguerite Henry (Macmillan)
Arabian Horses. Dorothy H. Patent (Holiday House)
Complete Book of Horses and Horsemanship. C. W. Anderson (Macmillan)
The Great Book of Horses. Catherine Dell (R. Rourke)
Guide to the Horses of the World. Caroline Silver (Exeter)
Horse Breeds and Breeding. Jane Kidd (Crescent)
Horse Happy: A Complete Guide to Owning Your Own Horse. Barbara J. Berry (Bobbs-Merrill)
The Horse and Pony Manual. David Hunt (Chartwell)
Horses and Riding. George Henschel (Franklin Watts)
The Ultimate Horse Book. Elwyn Hartley Edwards (Dorling Kindersley)

VIDEOS

The Art of Riding Series. (Visual Education Productions)
The Horse Family. (International Film Bureau)
Horses! (Encyclopedia Britannica)
The Mare and Foal. (Discovery Trail)
Nature: Wild Horses. (Warner Home Video)

PLACES TO WRITE

Here are some places to write for more information about horses. When you write, include your name and address, and be specific about the information you would like to receive. Don't forget to enclose a stamped, self-addressed envelope for a reply.

National Association for Humane
   and Environmental Education
P.O. Box 362
East Haddam, CT 06423-0362

Horse Council of British Columbia
5746B 176A Street
Cloverdale, British Columbia
V3S 4C7

Pennsylvania Horsebreeder's
   Association
701 East Baltimore Pike, Suite C1
Kennett Square, PA 19348

INDEX

Abbas Pasha 30
Andalusian horses 8, 29
Arabia 34
Arabians: and breeding
   standards 8, 34; colors of 10,
   38; as "daughters of the wind"
   13; and development of breed
   14; and endurance 34;
   introduction into Europe of
   29, 30; and longevity 28;
   origins of 10, 14, 29; physical
   characteristics of 5, 8, 13, 27,
   31, 32, 35; as racehorses 16;
   and stamina 14, 38
Asia 10

Bedouins 14, 34
brood mares 22

colts 32
crossbreeding 8, 29, 30, 38

Egypt 10, 29, 30
English thoroughbreds 8
Euphrates River 10

foals 6, 16, 28, 33, 36

France 29, 30

gallop 45

herd 13
highlands 10

Islam 29

King Solomon 10
King Wilhelm I 30

Lipizzaners 8
Louis XV 30

manes 8
mares 6, 7, 10, 13, 16, 22,
   28, 29, 30
Middle East 10
Muhammed 29

Napoleon 30
Nile River 10
North Africa 29

offspring 30

pace 34, 45

Spain 29
"Spanish eye" 40
stallions 14, 25, 29, 30, 40

thoroughbreds 6, 7, 8, 34
Trakehners 8